First Biographies

Florence Nightingale

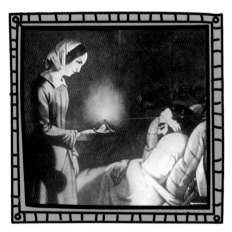

by Lola M. Schaefer and Wyatt Schaefer

Consulting Editor: Gail Saunders-Smith, PhD
Consultant: Veronica F. Rempusheski, PhD, RN, FAAN
Associate Professor, University of Kansas School of Nursing
Kansas City, Kansas

Capstone
press
Mankato, Minnesota

Pebble Books are published by Capstone Press,
151 Good Counsel Drive, P.O. Box 669, Mankato, Minnesota 56002.
www.capstonepress.com

1 2 3 4 5 6 09 08 07 06 05 04

Library of Congress Cataloging-in-Publication Data
Schaefer, Lola M., 1950–
    Florence Nightingale / by Lola M. Schaefer and Wyatt Schaefer.
    p. cm.—(First biographies)
    Includes bibliographical references and index.
    ISBN-13: 978-0-7368-2081-3 (hardcover)
    ISBN 0-7368-2081-7 (hardcover)
    ISBN-13: 978-0-7368-5083-4 (paperback)
    ISBN 0-7368-5083-X (paperback)
    1. Nightingale, Florence, 1820–1910—Juvenile literature. 2. Nurses—England—
Biography—Juvenile literature. [1. Nightingale, Florence, 1820–1910. 2. Nurses 3.
Women—Biography.] I. Schaefer, Wyatt S., 1978– II. Title. III. Series.
RT37.N5S336 2005
610.73′092—dc22   2003025606

Summary: Simple text and photographs present the life of Florence Nightingale, the
famous nurse and hospital reformist.

Note to Parents and Teachers

The First Biographies series supports national history standards for
units on people and culture. This book describes and illustrates the
life of Florence Nightingale. The photographs support early readers
in understanding the text. This book also introduces early readers
to subject-specific vocabulary words, which are defined in the
Glossary. Early readers may need assistance to read some words
and to use the Table of Contents, Glossary, Read More, Internet
Sites, and Index/Word List sections of the book.

Table of Contents

Time Line

1820
born

Early Life

Florence Nightingale was a nurse. She worked to make hospitals safe. She was born in Florence, Italy, in 1820. She was named after the city where she was born.

Florence, Italy, in the early 1800s
inset: Florence Nightingale around 1840

Time Line

1820	1825
born	moves to Embley Park

Florence grew up in England. She lived at Embley Park with her parents and sister. Her father taught Florence and her sister at home.

Embley Park, the Nightingale home, around 1910

Time Line

1820
born

1825
moves to
Embley Park

1851
attends nursing
school in Germany

Nursing

Florence wanted to become a nurse. In 1851, she went to a nursing school in Germany. She studied diseases and ways to help sick people.

nursing school in Kaiserworth, Germany

Time Line

1820
born

10

1825
moves to
Embley Park

1851
attends nursing
school in Germany

1853
runs hospital
in England

In 1853, Florence ran a hospital for women in London. She took care of many patients. She was good at her job.

Florence in 1855

Time Line

1820 born	1825 moves to Embley Park	1851 attends nursing school in Germany	1853 runs hospita in England

In 1854, Great Britain went to war with Russia. Hurt and sick soldiers needed help. Florence and 38 nurses took care of them in a war hospital in Turkey.

Florence awaiting patients during the Crimean War in 1855

1854–1856
helps soldiers in
Crimean War

Time Line

1820	1825	1851	1853
born	moves to	attends nursing	runs hospita
	Embley Park	school in Germany	in England

14

Florence and her nurses made the hospital clean and safe. They worked late at night by the light of their lamps. Soldiers called Florence the Lady with the Lamp.

1854–1856
helps soldiers in
Crimean War

Time Line

| 1820
born | 1825
moves to
Embley Park | 1851
attends nursing
school in Germany | 1853
runs hospito
in England |

Improving Hospitals

Florence returned to London after the war. She wrote letters to leaders in Great Britain. She told them how to make hospitals clean and safe.

1854–1856
helps soldiers in
Crimean War

Time Line

| 1820 born | 1825 moves to Embley Park | 1851 attends nursing school in Germany | 1853 runs hospit[al] in England |

18

In 1860, Florence opened a school for nurses. She wrote letters about nursing to students. She also wrote short books about nursing.

Florence (seated at center) with nurses in 1886

1854–1856
helps soldiers in
Crimean War

1860
opens school
for nurses

Time Line

1820	1825	1851	1853
born	moves to Embley Park	attends nursing school in Germany	runs hospi... in England

Florence died in London in 1910. People remember her as the Lady with the Lamp. They remember the ways she made hospitals safe.

Florence around 1891

1854–1856	1860	1910
helps soldiers in Crimean War	opens school for nurses	dies

Glossary

disease—an illness or sickness

hospital—a place where people go when they are sick or hurt

nurse—a person who takes care of people who are sick or hurt in a hospital

patient—a person in a hospital who is sick or hurt

soldier—a person who is in the army

Read More

Armentrout, David, and Patricia Armentrout.
Florence Nightingale. People Who Made a Difference.
Vero Beach, Fla.: Rourke, 2002.

Davis, Marc. *Florence Nightingale: Founder of the
Nightingale School of Nursing.* Our People.
Chanhassen, Minn.: Child's World, 2004.

Zemlicka, Shannon. *Florence Nightingale.* On My
Own Biography. Minneapolis: Carolrhoda, 2003.

Internet Sites

FactHound offers a safe, fun way to find Internet sites
related to this book. All of the sites on FactHound
have been researched by our staff.

Here's how:

1. Visit *www.facthound.com*

2. Type in this special code **0736820817** for
   age-appropriate sites. Or enter a search word
   related to this book for a more general search.

3. Click on the **Fetch It** button.

FactHound will fetch the best sites for you!

Index/Word List

Word Count: 228
Early-Intervention Level: 18

Editorial Credits

Martha E. H. Rustad, editor; Heather Kindseth, cover designer and illustrator; Enoch Peterson, production designer; Kelly Garvin, photo researcher; Karen Hieb, product planning editor

Photo Credits

Art Resource, NY/Alinari, 4
Corbis/Bettmann, 10, 14; Corbis/Stapleton Collection, 16; Corbis/Hulton-Deutsch Collection, 20
Country Joe's Tribute to Florence Nightingale, 8
Getty Images/Hulton Archive, cover, 1, 4 (inset), 6, 12, 18